Parent's Introduction

We Both Read is the first series of books designed to invite parents and children to share the reading of a story by taking turns reading aloud. This "shared reading" innovation, which was developed with reading education specialists, invites parents to read the more complex text and story line on the left-hand pages. Then, children can be encouraged to read the right-hand pages, which feature text written for a specific early reading level.

Reading aloud is one of the most important activities parents can share with their child to assist them in their reading development. However, *We Both Read* goes beyond reading *to* a child and allows parents to share the reading *with* a child. *We Both Read* is so powerful and effective because it combines two key elements in learning: "modeling" (the parent reads) and "doing" (the child reads). The result is not only faster reading development for the child, but a much more enjoyable and enriching experience for both!

You may find it helpful to read the entire book aloud yourself the first time, then invite your child to participate in the second reading. In some books, a few more difficult words will first be introduced in the parent's text, distinguished with **bold lettering**. Pointing out, and even discussing, these words will help familiarize your child with them and help to build your child's vocabulary. Also, note that a "talking parent" icon ⟲ precedes the parent's text, and a "talking child" icon ⟲ precedes the child's text.

We encourage you to share and interact with your child as you read the book together. If your child is having difficulty, you might want to mention a few things to help him. "Sounding out" is good, but it will not work with all words. Children can pick up clues about the words they are reading from the story, the context of the sentence, or even the pictures. Some stories have rhyming patterns that might help. It might also help them to touch the words with their finger as they read, to better connect the voice sound and the printed word.

Sharing the *We Both Read* books together will engage you and your child in an interactive adventure in reading! It is a fun and easy way to encourage and help your child to read—and a wonderful way to start them off on a lifetime of reading enjoyment!

We Both Read: Soccer!

———————————————————————————————

Text Copyright © 2010 by Dev Ross
Illustrations Copyright © 2010 by David Wenzel
Use of photographs provided by Fotosearch and Getty Images © 2010

We Both Read® is a trademark of Treasure Bay, Inc.

Published by
Treasure Bay, Inc.
P. O. Box 119
Novato, CA 94948 USA

Printed in Singapore

Library of Congress Catalog Card Number: 2009930964

Hardcover ISBN-13: 978-1-60115-239-8
Paperback ISBN-13: 978-1-60115-240-4

We Both Read® Books
Patent No. 5,957,693

Visit us online at:
www.webothread.com

PR 11-09

Soccer!

By Dev Ross

with illustrations by David Wenzel

TREASURE BAY

   Do you love the game of soccer? If your answer is "Yes!" then you are not alone. Millions of people around the world love soccer. It is widely considered to be the most popular sport on the planet. There is a soccer confederation on every continent except Antarctica. (It's hard to play on all that ice!)

   In the United States, the game is called "soccer." In many other countries, it's called "football." No matter what it's called, it's a terrific game. It's fun to watch and even more fun to play.

3

   Games **similar** to the modern game of soccer have been around for **thousands** of years. Ancient Chinese writings from around 50 B.C. describe a soccer-like game in which the players kicked around a leather ball filled with hair. The goal was to kick the ball into a net held up by bamboo canes. The game was played to celebrate the emperor's birthday.

A **similar** game was played in Japan over one **thousand** years ago. Players kicked a ball back and forth, trying to keep it from touching the ground. In modern soccer, the ball can touch the ground. However, it cannot touch arms or hands.

Long ago, in the country now known as Italy, the Romans also played a game much like soccer. However, instead of eleven players on a team, they had twenty-seven. These players played so intensely that many of them had to be carried off the field on stretchers!

One of the oldest forms of the game was played by Native Americans. They played this game over six thousand years ago. The game was not played with a leather ball. It was played with a round stone.

Despite its **international** appeal, soccer was not always loved by everyone. Seven hundred years ago, King Edward of England thought the game was much too noisy and vulgar. So, the king passed laws that would put anyone who played soccer in jail. However, even the threat of imprisonment could not stop people from playing the game they adored.

During the time of King Edward, the game was played with very few rules. Players sometimes got into fights.

In 1863, the rules of the game were finally set. Today, most soccer teams around the world play by the rules of the **International** Football Association Board.

The World Cup is a worldwide soccer contest played by men's national soccer teams. This **championship** has been played every four years since 1930. The final game of the playoffs is the most watched sporting event in the world.

In 1991, professional female soccer players joined in competing too. The Women's World **Championship** is also played every four years.

Kids don't have to wait four years to play in soccer **championships**. Local **championships** for young players are held every year at the end of soccer season. These games can be just as exciting as the world class games. The winning teams often win big trophies!

 One of the world's most famous soccer players was a Brazilian named **Pelé**. During twenty-two years of playing professional soccer, **Pelé** scored 1,281 goals. At age seventeen, he was the youngest player ever to play in the World Cup finals. **Pelé** was such a great player that once, during a war in Nigeria, both sides stopped fighting just so they could watch **Pelé** play!

When **Pelé** was a young boy, his family did not have much money. He and his friends would make their own soccer ball by stuffing a sock with newspaper. They often played the game in their bare feet. They called their team "The Shoeless Ones."

Mia Hamm was the best-known female American soccer player of the 1990s. When she was fifteen years old, Mia became the youngest woman ever to make the U.S. national soccer team. Mia's team won gold medals at the 1996 and 2004 Olympics, and she helped her team claim the 1999 Women's World Cup. In 2007, Mia Hamm was elected to the U.S. National Soccer Hall of Fame.

When Mia was a little girl, she was very good at playing sports. Her older brother used her as a "secret weapon" when they played Capture the Flag with their friends. The secret was that she could run really fast! Being a strong runner is an important part of playing soccer.

   Soccer is played on a rectangular field with net goals on either side of the field. Though soccer teams can have both boys and girls on them, most soccer teams have either all boys or all girls. Each team member is given a special position to play. One player is the **goalie,** while the other ten players are outfielders, who play defensive, midfield, and attacking positions.

Each team tries to send the ball into the net on the other side of the field. A player may do this by using any part of the body except the arms and hands. The **goalie** is the only player who may use arms or hands. The **goalie's** job is to stop the other team from getting the ball into the net.

Whether you're a professional soccer player or playing just for fun, it is important to wear the correct soccer gear. Shin guards are needed to protect the legs. Cleats are worn as footwear to avoid slipping on a grassy field. It is also important to use a **properly inflated** soccer ball.

 **"Properly inflated"** means that the ball has just the right amount of air, so it is not too hard or too soft. The soccer balls used today are made from rubber and leather. But long ago, soccer balls were often made from the bladders of animals.

 Soccer balls come in different sizes. Players under eight years old usually use a size 3 ball. Players between eight and twelve usually use a size 4 ball, and players over twelve usually use a size 5 ball. Many beginning soccer players prefer a softer ball. Once they've gained experience, they tend to favor a harder ball.

 Members of a soccer team usually wear a special uniform. Along with cleats and shin guards, they wear special shorts that let them run and jump. Goalies wear special soccer gloves to protect their hands.

Soccer drills help players **improve** their skills. The Magic Hop drill helps them **improve** their ability to stop the ball. To do the Magic Hop, players might first practice skipping. Next, with the ball slowly rolling forward, they put one foot beside the ball, then hop up. While they're in the air, they lightly tap the top of the ball with their other foot and then keep moving forward to land on the same foot. Your soccer coach can show you how to do this.

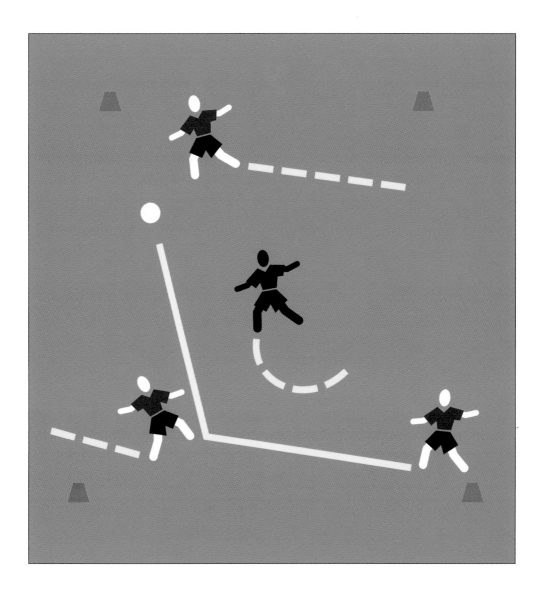

The Pig-in-the-Middle drill helps **improve** passing skills. It's also good practice for taking the ball away from the other team. Three players stand in a triangle with the "pig" in the center. The three players on the outside pass the ball to each other while the "pig" tries to take it away. Try this one with your friends!

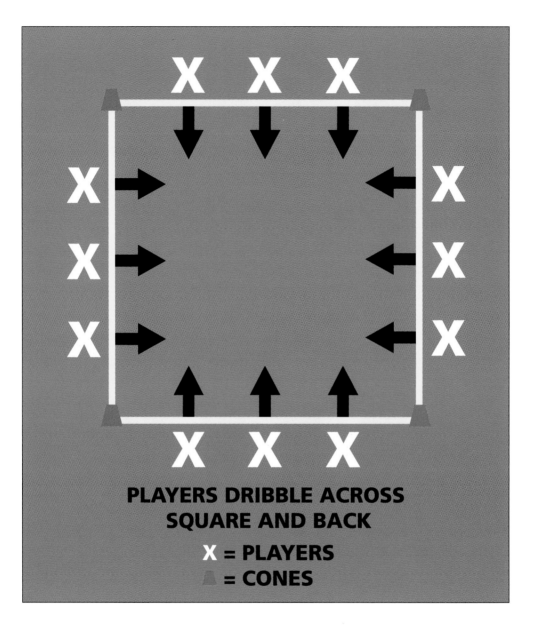

**PLAYERS DRIBBLE ACROSS
SQUARE AND BACK**

X = PLAYERS
= CONES

Dribbling across a Square is a drill that can help improve your dribbling skills. First, mark out an imaginary square, and have your teammates stand in different positions all around the square. On "Go!" start dribbling across the square, trying not to bump anyone. The more you practice, the more controlled your dribbling will become.

 A cone drill can be used to improve your control of the ball. Space out cones or markers in a long line. Start at one end, and weave the ball back and forth through the markers until you reach the other end.

Anyone can have a bad game. Sometimes, even famous soccer players don't play as well as they would like to. It's important to remember that we all make mistakes. Making mistakes is part of learning to play soccer. Try not to be too hard on yourself and, most importantly, have a good time.

 To improve your soccer game, you must get on the field and practice. It is also good to practice the game inside your head. Relax, close your eyes, and imagine dribbling the ball down the field. Now imagine kicking it into the goal!

Every sport has its own special vocabulary. In soccer, to "carry" the ball means to dribble. To "chip" the ball means to kick it over the heads of the other team. If the **referee** blows the whistle and says "hand ball," it means someone touched the ball illegally with his arms or hands.

 Soccer **referees** are there to make sure that the rules of the game are followed. It's their job to ensure that every game played is safe, fair, and fun. To do their job well, they must insist that all players behave properly.

   When a referee holds up a yellow card, it is a warning to a player who has behaved badly. If the referee holds up a red card, the offending player must leave the field and may no longer play in the game.

The best way to avoid a red or yellow card is to always display good **sportsmanship**.

 Good **sportsmanship** means treating all the players with respect. It means playing by the rules. It means not yelling at the other team or at your own teammates. It can be as simple as shaking hands after the game, whether you win or lose.

Soccer is a cooperative sport. It takes teamwork to win a game. So don't be a ball hog! Knowing how to work together and **support** your teammates helps you play well and have more fun. Teamwork also works off the soccer field. Teamwork helps at home, with your friends, and at school.

Cheering for your teammates is fun. You can tell them "Way to go!" and **support** them by calling out, "Win the ball!" Soccer crowds can also encourage players with their cheers. "Play hard, play fair, have FUN!" is a popular cheer.

Some soccer moves performed by very skilled players are
absolutely fantastic to see. The bicycle kick is one of them.
In this move, players kick the ball backwards over their own
head, and send it into the goal. This kick is very difficult and
dangerous to perform. Don't try it yourself!

 Soccer players should always warm up before playing. Warming up prepares the body to play hard. Some people like to jog to warm up. Some teams gently dribble the ball around the field. Both are great ways to get the body moving.

 Soccer players need a healthy diet to **fuel** their bodies for high **performance** during the game. It is best to eat a meal that includes whole grains, fruit, and vegetables one or two hours before the game starts. Be sure to also drink plenty of water before, during, and after the game!

What you eat after the game is important too. A healthy after-game snack will help your body **fuel** up again. Junk food may taste good, but it can really slow your **performance**. Watermelon slices and whole grain snack bars are better choices than cookies and chips.

The American Youth Soccer Organization (AYSO) is a soccer program dedicated to bringing fun soccer experiences to kids ages four to eighteen. AYSO has more than 50,000 teams and more than 650,000 players. If you are interested in playing soccer for the first time, or joining a team, contact your community's AYSO.

AYSO also trains people to coach soccer teams. Soccer coaches teach the rules of the game and run practice drills. They give pointers on how to dribble, pass, and kick the ball into the goal. A good coach can help you become the best soccer player you can be.

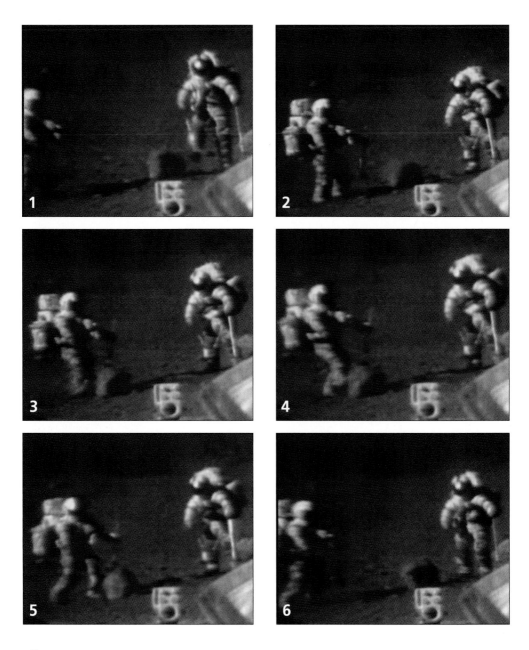

Though soccer is a fast game, there is one place where it must be played slowly. And that's on the moon! During an Apollo 17 lunar landing, two astronauts began kicking a large moon rock like it was a soccer ball. Since there's a lot less gravity on the moon, kicking big rocks there is a lot easier than here on Earth!

It's exciting to run down the field with the ball. It's a thrill to kick the ball into the goal. And watching a soccer game is almost as exciting as playing the game. It's easy to see why soccer is so popular all around the world!

If you liked *Soccer!*, here is another
We Both Read® book you are sure to enjoy!

Endangered Animals

This book takes a close look at various animals from
around the world that are in danger of becoming
extinct. It discusses how the animals have become
endangered due to worldwide threats, including pollution,
deforestation, and global warming. Featuring stunning
photographs of many endangered animals in their
natural habitats, the book also relates some of the
positive steps being taken to protect the animals and
explains how we can all take part in saving them.

To see all the We Both Read books that are available,
just go online to **www.webothread.com**.